A Note to Parents and Teachers

DK READERS is a compelling reading programme for children, designed in conjunction with leading literacy experts, including Cliff Moon M.Ed., Honorary Fellow of the University of Reading. Cliff Moon has spent many years as a teacher and teacher educator specializing in reading and has written more than 140 books for children and teachers. He reviews regularly for teachers' journals.

Beautiful illustrations and superb full-colour photographs combine with engaging, easy-to-read stories to offer a fresh approach to each subject in the series. Each DK READER is guaranteed to capture a child's interest while developing his or her reading skills, general knowledge, and love of reading.

The five levels of DK READERS are aimed at different reading abilities, enabling you to choose the books that are exactly right for your child:

Pre-level 1 – Learning to read
Level 1   – Beginning to read
Level 2   – Beginning to read alone
Level 3   – Reading alone
Level 4   – Proficient readers

The "normal" age at which a child begins to read can be anywhere from three to eight years old, so these levels are only a general guideline.

No matter which level you select, you can be sure that you are helping your child learn to read, then read to learn!

LONDON, NEW YORK, MUNICH,
MELBOURNE, AND DELHI

Series Editor Deborah Lock
Senior Art Editor Tory Gordon-Harris
Design Assistant Sadie Thomas
Production Claire Pearson
DTP Designer Almudena Díaz

Reading Consultant
Cliff Moon, M.Ed.

Published in Great Britain by Dorling Kindersley Limited
80, The Strand, London, WC2R ORL
8 10 9 7

A Penguin Company

A CIP record for this book is available
from the British Library

ISBN 978-0-7513-1390-1

Colour reproduction by Colourscan, Singapore
Printed and bound in China by L Rex Printing Co., Ltd.

The publisher would like to thank the following for their kind
permission to reproduce their photographs:
a=above; c=centre; b=below; l=left; r=right t=top;

Ardea London Ltd: 23tr; **Corbis:** Wolfgang Kaehler 13c. Rob C.
Nunnington/Gallo Images 28tl; **Philip Dowell:** 26-27; **Getty Images:**
Arthur S.Aubry 30-31; Geoff du Feu 10tl; David McGlynn 4cl; Laurence
Monneret 31c; Tom Schierlitz 27br; Bob Stefko 18l; Kevin Summers
20-21; **Natural History Museum:** 2cra, 7cbr, 24bl, 24br, 25bl, 25bc,
25bcr, 32tl, 32bl; **N.H.P.A:** Stephen Dalton 15tr; David Middleton
4-5; **Oxford Scientific Film:** 8tl, 8-9, 9tc, Claude Steelman/SAL 6-7;
Jerry Young: 11bc, 26bl; **Getty Images:** Front cover: Steve Satushek

All other images © Dorling Kindersley
For further imformation see: www.dkimages.com

see our complete catalogue at
www.dk.com

DK READERS

LEARNING
pre-level **1** TO READ

Garden
Friends

A Dorling Kindersley Book

butterfly

garden

Meet the small animals in my garden.

nail

5

antenna

flower

butterflies

Hello, butterfly.
You are resting
on a flower.

wing

leaf

eye

mouth

 caterpillars

Hello, caterpillar.
You are eating
a big leaf.

spot

 ladybirds

Hello, ladybirds.
How many spots
do you have?

head

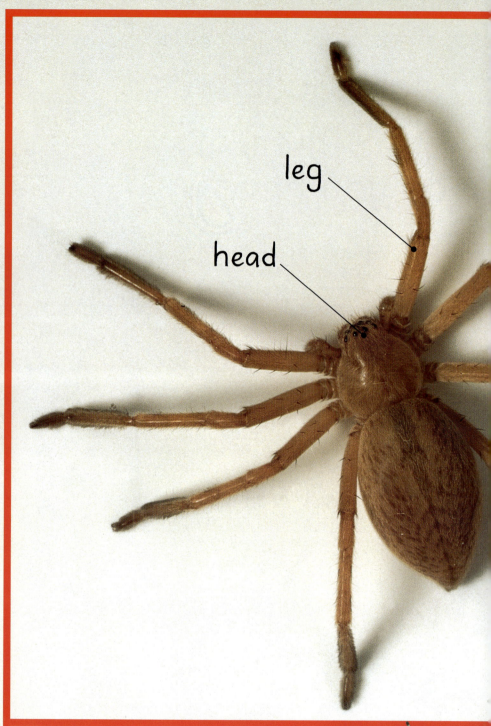

leg

head

 spiders

Hello, spider.
You have spun
a big web.

web

flower

furry body

Hello, bumblebee.
You are drinking
from a flower.

Hello, centipede.
How many legs
do you have?

centipedes

head

leg

Hello, dragonfly.
You are flying
around very fast.

dragonflies

wing

leg

baby snail

shell

snails

Hello, snail.
You have a baby
on your back.

soft body

worms

Hello, worms.
Which one is
the longest?

Hello, stag beetle. You have very sharp jaws.

wing

 beetles

head

jaw

25

Hello, frogs.
You are hiding
in the grass.

foot

frogs

grasshoppers

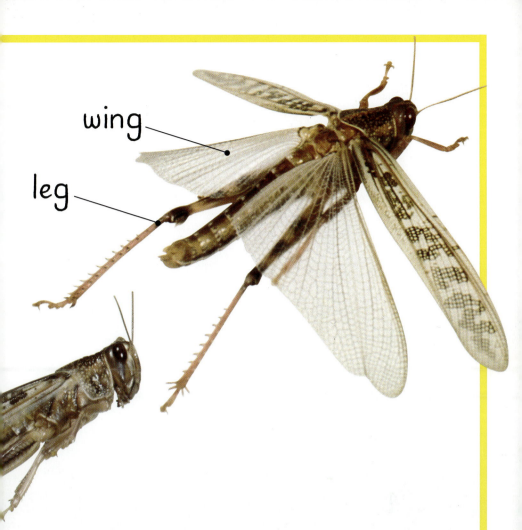

wing

leg

Hello, grasshoppers.
Wow!
What a big jump!

dragonfly

 Which animals are

in your garden?

Picture word list

 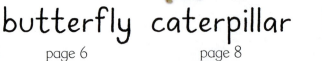

butterfly
page 6

caterpillar
page 8

ladybird
page 10

spider
page 12

bumblebee
page 14

centipede
page 16

dragonfly
page 18

snail
page 20

worm
page 22

beetle
page 24

frog
page 26

grasshopper
page 28